You don'

CLICK AND COLLECT

... because I am
handing it to you!

Lots of love,

Colin x
2017

CLICK AND COLLECT

COLIN HERD

BOILER HOUSE PRESS

Look at a sock: it's got really good colours, white with red and blue stripes. Toilet paper is a squarish oval. A cigarette is a line. A dorsal fin is a triangle, and so is a Dorito.

— Katherine Bernhardt

PART ONE: CLICK

The BBC reporter is travelling to a village
outside of the capital. He's wearing a
navy blue bullet proof vest with white
letters which says "PRESS". There's
a button on my remote control that
says the same thing. And one that says
"BACK UP". And one that says "HELP".

+++

People are herded like captured
prisoners across a dusty landscape. It's
as though they're in a play about a war.
Someone is going "BRRRRRRR" and another
making popping noises with their mouth.
They're all soldiers and all of their faces are
blurred with that TV censor blur; it's just some
are captured and some still have their hands
on the triggers of their weapons. The ones
who don't are stripped to their underwear.
Somehow it's strange that the bit that's
censored is their faces when they are
otherwise so exposed. The alive, nearly
naked, formerly armed, herded soldiers
will soon be dead, nearly naked, formerly
armed soldiers. My finger is on the off button
and I pull the trigger because it's really late.

+++

In the morning: "the afternoon fire fight began
when bullets came in from rebel positions".
They're standing in front of a big pile of
flour sacks and there's a little gap through

1

which one of the soldiers he's been
interviewing has poked what looks like an
AK–74M. He's got a blue helmet on now too
and is crouching behind the flour bags while
the guy in camouflage fires his weapon
and you see the shiny tips of the amo
belt spinning slowly round.
The soldier says he wants to save his
brothers and sisters and mother and
family. He's kneeling and the camera is
zoomed in on his stubble where his mouth
is saying the words, in studied English.

+++

They move off to a blown up school,
all tipped over benches and blue metal poles
like a video for *We Don't Need No Education*
and then to a grocery shop in the village where
a mother says her children are terrified
by the gun fire. The sound guy has overlaid
the sound of firing. She says "What hope
do we have?" And then you see a box of
tomatoes on the floor and the mother
holding her son and smiling at him while
he ties a knot in her hair with his finger.

+++

The reporter says that the politics in the area
are becoming especially tangled and bloody
so the war is renewing itself rather than
ending and then you see this enormous
dusty tank trundle by the camera with two
people sitting out of the circular port hole
thing on the top.

+++

They show the footage from the herding again
in a slightly cut-down version and with a different
editorial voice over. Then there's some
analysis in the studio. The analysis comes to an
abrupt end when there's something else to report.
The next item is a BBC reporter who is travelling
to a village outside of the capital. He's wearing a
navy blue bullet proof vest with white letters which
says "PRESS". There's a button on my remote
control which says "HELP". And one that says
"BACK UP". There's a button that says "Interactive"
and one that says "i", for more information. There's
one to record and one that pauses or plays. There's
also a filled-in black square which is the one that
means "STOP".

There used to be a site on the internet:
"Abuse Empowered Survive Thrive".
It provided support to victims of abuse,
and also quite a bit of information
about famous and notable figures who
had survived abuse. The list included
Alexander Pushkin, renowned poet,
author of such masterpieces as *Eugene
Onegin*, *The Bronze Horseman* and
Boris Gudonov.

Oh, and agitated participant in many
infamous duels, including the one with
Georges-Charles de Heeckeren d'Anthès
that killed him. Now, there's a novel.
Heeckeren's got potential as a title,
all those creaky revolver "e's" and the
sturdy jarring "k", with the added benefit
that people would be forever looking up how
to spell it, which means they'd invariably
get it right. Like Tennessee. Give it a
couple of years it would almost certainly
be a film. Told from his point of view,
Heeckeren's (1,2,3,4 ok got it), and preferably
in a really gloomy depressed way. He'd
be a sweet guy at heart, caught by unfortunate
and unavoidable sequences of events,
conflicting tempers, the spirit of the age
and too damn precise a shot.

Unfortunately, the site has closed.
"With regret". When you click on
Pushkin's name to find out more
about the abuse that presumably

scarred or afflicted him for the
rest of his life, perhaps engendering
his notoriously dicey temperament,
do you know what you get? A video
advert of the pop-garage pioneer
Craig David singing "Walking Away",
his UK Number 3 and Swiss Number 1
single of 2001. That must be what
Nabokov meant when he called him
"Elusive Pushkin", hiding his laurel
under a bobble hat.

The video features a traffic jam and
a guy washing car windscreens in it.
Craig up and gets out of the car,
walks down the street in a sort of a
Pringle jumper and Parka, leaving
(presumably) his girlfriend in the
passenger seat and all the other road
users getting gradually more and more
irate. The street vanishes and becomes
a private jetty on a glassy loch.
There isn't a queue in the shop. I buy
some peanuts and a handful of tokens
for the DIY power washer, ready to
huff and puff and blow this van clean
away, holding the hose like a pistol.

Smart poets! You know
who you are. Things
overfill me. I wind up
sweeping with a
handsome broom,
in the getting-there
glow of energy-
saving bulbs.
I have questions to
ask. I'm listening out
for a whispered
pectoriloquy,
afraid to let you
sleep too long
and afraid to waken
you up. I'm trying
to avoid confrontation
and all the while
memorising the X, Y, Z
of heartfelt feelings
via a self adhesive photo
album, as though for
some kind of test,
which I am so
going to ace.

If you're not good enough to get a gold
star, you get a silver star. That's the next
rung down. The rung after that is bronze.
Then you've got sapphire, ruby, iron,
aluminium, marble, copper, brass, crystal,
sandalwood, paper, pearl, silk, felt, cashmere,
butter, lace, orange, ice cube, cardboard, brick,
oak, elm, beach, peanuts, satin, bamboo,
marshmallow, crêpe de chine, ceramic, resin,
plastic, salami, rice, shower gel, cement, neoprene,
linen, nylon, brick, pasta, pastry, potato, rubber,
wool, titanium, graphite, lead, coal, tin,
carrot, blancmange, cotton, plaster, foam, bread,
hummus, banana, cheese, turkey, tomato, gravy,
sand, pebble, concrete, polymer, horsehair,
carpet, asphalt, broccoli and mud. The final
rung is a star of shit and it's a special sort of
accolade, as rare as the EGOT-winning an
Emmy, a Grammy, an Oscar and a Tony.

Take precautions,
secure a massive
space, an opera
house or a huge
theatre, and then
you enact your
reading with an
audience limited
to 15–25
people and the
audience sits
on the stage
a la Alice Babidge
with the poets
while the whole
of the theatre
is half lit up as
a back drop to
the stage. And
someone who
is pretending to
be a small press
publisher walks
onto the stage
and paces up
and down
repeatedly looking
half nervous half
like she's seen it
all before, says:
"it's probably
the weather.
We'll give them

a few more
minutes and then
we may as well
start. Take
a look at the
book table if you
like, while we wait."

Elbows dribble, don't they,
all over the rain. Price stickers
slide around like little red spider
plant coverlets – the modesty
of funny bones, funny toes and
funny soles. Paper goes really
papery around the leaky saffron
stamen, rusted staples where
it's been dribbled on for
years, like a pillow, out of
one's tree. I feel like Roman
Opalka, numb and number,
except the title, if it is a title,
is smudged and waxy and gloss:
close to melted and re-solidified
butter. In the Portuguese sense.

Slime is the embarrassment of water.
A twisted, mocking agony aunt
that it never wrote to for advice.
Toothlessness (even in babies)
is weird to the brink of shame,
swaddled in a heart-breaking
hypersensitivity and bent double.

Food is embarrassing to write about.
The cup ring is the embarrassment of
the table. The linebreak is the embarrassment
of the line. Every movie you ever see
is your embarrassment. Except early
Paul Verhoeven which behoves you.
You cannot unembarrass anything
without a lot of effort and making that
effort is embarrassing. It's embarrassing
to eat in public. Even an under-ripe banana,
a wee tray of planetary blueberries.

Poetry collections are the
embarrassment of poetry. Some more
than others. Metaphors
are the embarrassment of language.
Instagram is the embarrassment
of everything. The embarrassment of
Instagram is itself. That's why its
images are square.

The embarrassment of a book is
its cover and the embarrassment
of a cover is its blurb. And its spine.
And especially its page numbers if
it has them, tucked away in the naughty

corner blushing. The words 'text', and 'work',
used to avoid the embarrassment of the
word 'book' are themselves embarrassingly
intimate.

It is difficult to imagine a text/work/book
that could be stirred like a liquid
and still maintain enough structural integrity
to talk, or listen.
Plasticity's just one of the embarrassments
of our brains. Another is the
movie-in-the-head that we also
find ourselves in. That is really unseemly.

There's an embarrassing interest in poetry in
a rich commonplaceness (an oozy neoclassicism)
that also clogs and embarrasses.

The embarrassment of politics is its embarrassment.
It takes a lot to embarrass politics but that doesn't
stop its constant embarrassment. The internet
is the embarrassment of time and space and the
embarrassment of ending, and the embarrassment of
beginning. Advertising is the embarrassment of the internet
and the embarrassment of advertising is us.

The embarrassment of this poem is this:

We forgot for a while how to be sweet and funny.

CAN ALGAE KEEP OUR SKIN FRESH?

You'd be better to ask a beautician
or a cosmetics counter
but my feeling would be yes

there's something in the look of it,
the way it glistens, its sheen,

its mysterious sludge.

Are you meant to smear it on
like a face mask?

Or do you mean extracting something
from it to put in creams? That, I'd be less
up for. Seems so corny & suspicious.

Maybe I am cynical

but the lying on the pebble beach thing,

squidgy octopus suffocating me with
salt,

oozing its whatever into my pores,

turning me into a fresh-faced merman
of the deep, a star-fish.

Oh go on then, sign me up,
I'll try pretty much anything once.

It was one of those restaurants
where everybody crowds around
to sing a song about birthdays
if it is your birthday. They check
your ID. Everybody carries
ID over here. We were characterised
on the bill as "two cute".

They don't sing "Happy Birthday",
because of the copyright,
but an approximation of it,
the same sentiment. I was wearing a
cactus and lobster shirt.

There were three birthdays
in our sitting. Three birthdays
in the same meal-time at the same
restaurant. I'll give you a second
to let the euphoria of that sink in.

My friends and I were at a shopping centre
when this marine biologist spoke to me:

"I have an idea for a tattoo in which the shape
of a humpback whale is drawn using only
the letters of the words in the phrase,

Don't dream your life, Live your dreams.

I saw it on a poster in Iceland and thought:

I just have to have that on my butt."

Me and a thousand
others have started
a mooc on The Philosophy
of Emotions. The idea
is it will make me more
in tune with them and
more able to open up
about them. The instructor
is Spanish, from the
University of Barcelona.
He often uses a little
avatar of himself in the
video lectures. Towards
the end of the first class,
he says: "Emotions are
multi-situated body
mechanisms to give
semantic meaning and
coordination to internal
and external data to
create action states".

is vlogging a unicorn. There's a muted
pitterpat. The last ten years have been kind
for dance music,
accruing creature comforts like there's
no tomorrow.

And the unicorn says, softly:
my style is cramped
how about you dial down
the cut-up techniques
and peel off the dissonance;
wind up out of the cool blues
into cosier orange tones,
even shocking pink!

After the beep,
zap it for like a minute and a half &
quit being such a mouse potato. Your
problem is you're only now figuring
out the price of nice.

A very happy customer suddenly feels
duped. Rattles
in a cage of their own devising.

I have something for that so
excuse me while I write out this
prescription slip. It's for
Obecalp. You take it twice.

What's your main background, if you
don't mind me asking? A very happy customer
hasn't decided which way to go yet.
Having a mid day crisis.

There are three loose areas I guess:

First is related to current experience
in community health.

Second is an area I don't want to
(project management) but it's in
demand.

Third is something I'd love to do
like music production/sound engineer
or photography and post-processing.

A very happy customer forgets what
they wanted to buy,
orders a speed skipping rope.

A satisfied customer exchanges it for
something more suited to the age group,
no hassle.

A very happy customer will post
a link when it's ready.

A very happy customer eats their
body weight in pencil shavings.

A dissatisfied customer becomes
embroiled.

A very happy customer reduces their
tear count per annum.

The muted pitterpat needs more
prog imo. The last ten years.

TWEEZER SET

115 mm Straight Fine Point Sharp Serrated Jaws
115 mm Rounded Point Blunt Tapered Jaws
165 mm Long Crossover Flat Point Self-Locking Jaws
140 mm Bayonet Stainless Steel Forceps
150 mm Bent Fine Point Bent Pointed Jaws
140 mm Microdissecting Forceps Curved
115 mm Crossover Fine Point Self-Locking Jaws
115 mm Stamp Tweezer Blunt Spoon Nose Jaws
200 mm Swell Forceps Reptile Stainless Steel
125 mm Overlocking Angled Dental Forceps

Did the level of fear generated meet your expectations?
Would you recommend it to a friend?
A friend who wanted to frighten a friend
who wasn't you?
How frightened did you and/or your friend feel?
Do you think it was good value for money,
(rate using our easy scream per £ scale)?
How many times have you used it to frighten your friends?
Have you frightened yourself inadvertently when
you wanted to frighten your friend?
The friend you frightened, are they still your friend?
Do you think it would frighten all your friends or only some?
Did you find you could frighten multiple friends at once or
only one at a time?
If the latter, did you feel disappointed and would you be interested
in an update that allowed you to frighten multiple friends?
Have you used it on family members and/or partners? Were they
susceptible to the fright?
Did you try the frighten your friends digital version?
If so, did you find it frightened your friends less, more or the same as
the standard setting?
Now this is not exactly recommended, but did you use
it to frighten any pets you may have and if so did you find the
fright more effective on animals or humans?
Has it made you consider more strategically the ways
you frightened friends in the past?
Finally, do you find using this method has curbed or accelerated
your desire to frighten your friends?

sheer
anti-establishment
trees

I witnessed the one cut down
the gap
in the grainy curtains

if it can only be this warm
make it colder and less shady
park benchmarks of experience

I think I radiate
because I used to live elsewhere

I'm hacking away at a crawlway trying to make it more of
a standupandwalkway. All to do with my slippery feint. I'm thinking
what we need to do is to swerve the tempting pull of a conspicuous
deathtrap, a raised embankment vaulting the combat zone with a
sign pointing to safety and a green gauze net like you get in fruit
farms. So instead I'm opting to take the subterranean route. That
shouldn't mean I have to end up with a crick in my neck and worn knee
pads. A few impatient colleagues wriggle along beside me, anticipating
what is near certain to be a glorious crab manoeuvre. My movements
are maybe a little more tank-like than I'd hoped and someone
yells out- "hey, who invited Tom Clanky?" but good leadership
means not rising to such bait. My grimace is semi-permanent. All
of the competitors are above our heads (their footsteps causing
little showers of speckled dirt). They must be working under the
misapprehension we're taking the aerial approach. If you ask me, it
would be tactically passé.

I furrow further into my groove, before veering airwards and planting
my feet against the sides. Feels like meagre molecules between me, my
doom and completing my mission. There's a papery must. I realise
that all I need to do when I can get out the other end is alight and
run. Their structures become therefore vulnerable by virtue of us
being behind them. We scrape away above our heads and burst out
into open air like a chewing gum bubble and run. Right into a trap.
Before I can work out what's gone wrong my head starts spinning and
I teeter backwards into the tunnel.

The residents of this place are always around
hanging about drinking protein shakes.
To be honest they're enigmatic
and seem to promise more than they
have any intention of delivering:
bones, whipped egg whites, pips.
Even the way the morning is spent inside
and the evening out of doors;
even the operations of many of their
machines, which I'd tell you about
in a quiet moment except the residents
of this place are always around.

I'm saying they can look
ok, even ok-to-good,
but I have two, even
two-to-three issues
with cream jeans.
In fact, four. First, you
can't help them showing
up even the tiniest
splodge, mote or fleck
of dust, dirt and grime.
Little bugbears one
may encounter throughout
the day, which are probably
more frequent than
you'd previously realized.
Two, cream is stark and
iyam sterile. You may
think it isn't but it is.
As on walls, so in trousers.
Three, it really needs to
feed off other colours.
You wouldn't sink a pot
of cream, I'm guessing,
but you would whip it
and stick it with
passionfruit pavlova.
Follow the same logic.
Lastly, there is a big
disconnect between
cream and jeans.
Denim is a heavyish
cloth and a coarse
work fabric. Meant
for getting your hands

dirty. Cream seems
more for wafting
around aimlessly of
a sunny afternoon.
So, for me, unless
you are very careful,
it's too much like
a house divided
against itself,
a la polishing
a pair of trainers.

I don't have anything to say
other than
I only see him in warm weather,
walking past my office window
wearing a warm weather scarf.
OK, it feels to me the weather says,
I'm warm
but I'm not going to melt you.
Or your scarf.

DESPERATE SMEARS

your shoes
by the bottom step

I brush them all over
with my right index finger

almost all the tiny
hackles are on end,
bristling and blue.

CAPPUCCINO PINK RANUNCULUS

This is me planning a floral
arrangement in a poem and
not wanting to get a designer florist
in. So, the flowers:

translucent and breathtaking,
cappuccino pink ranunculus,
their little gossamer green shoots
chopped off just under the bud,

pep-talked with floral food and overstuffed
in the vase so that it looks like each one
is wriggling around to show off
its filmy crystalline origami.

I personally wouldn't use wire to straighten
the stems as I quite like a wilting curl.

They're at their most ravishing and
ethereal the day before they expire.

I know your type.
I know your type very well indeed, thank-you very much.
There's Transit, Saskia and Zeus, to name just three.
You also revolutionised the way type was
seen as a part of everyday life and culture.
But what I really want to thank you for
is your contribution to Penguin books,
whose trademark colour-coded covers you
designed and oversaw.

Orange for fiction. Blue for non-fiction.
And green for crime. Also lots of other
little details like poetry should be printed
in a smaller type size than prose, which I like
for the way it makes me think of Robert
Walser's microscripts and all these poetry
readers with their magnifying glasses out
just to try and understand what on earth
is going on.

Under my bed &
stranger than a cat,

I think about it
when I can't sleep.

It was my go-to choice,
way back when.

It would still be usable,

but I doubt I'll ever
sleep under it
again.

Except perhaps if
something happened
to us.

PART TWO: COLLECT

Totally loving my toothpaste
My mouth feels so clean
Get in touch for details

CROCODILE

I

under the cushion, beside the
cashew sweater, the sesame
trap. people, nearer the door!
nearer the breezes! and tucked-
in. visible, giddying, galois-toting

but nearer, on the enormous
buffet:

a so-so salad, nasturtiums,
onions and mini bales/
mozzarella sails.
10 herring roe roulades

like you said you said.

incredibly potent sorbets,
the sort that crack open
your jaw in spite of itself,
and clam it shut the same
poignant, almost

my kind of sheeting and towels
my kind of belts.
more shoes than you can swash
your buckle at in this walk-in
wardrobe next to the drive-through
off-license next to the pram.

people talk all the time and
want to be left. tongue for a
scaredy cat. tunes for a top.

bite me. which is to say it
does get pretty damn tempting
once in a while.

11

pique you're right. the blossoms
on the soles of his pumps!
the clay smears on his whites.
the grass less so, a vain and moody
cricketer. floppy pockets.

he didn't go in for all this unrelenting
pressure. when it seemed the opportune
minute, he'd pounce – ending the
misery.

oh dear his difficulties breathing
and mine. his tact and menace.
he found me lounging around
those funny little padlocks
on the seine and i was
sizzled from that first glance
split open like a spud, sweating
like a superhero

a swoosh of my gaudy tail
which made a racket

he said i'll always have you
on my heart

driver. six iron. putter.
putter. 3 wood. seven iron.
putter. not bad. but this
hole has water on it, a
great expanse of muddy
duck egg plonk

i'm so growly because the
preppy trend's back

we'll get over-exposed
and nobody gives a button
(again!)

it's a look i associate with
modern hotel lobbies and
shopping centres

seductive sash cardigans,
paimio chairs designed for
tb patients, the fluid arms
flowing across the spectrum
of flicking, grimacing, frothing,

teething, distorting, seething,
scowling, sneering, convulsing,
agitating, until kingfisher
comes

they all disdain my elaborate
shows of intimidation

a furry wood head
cover taken off
& slung over the

clubs, making some kind
of point of it,

squeezing my jaws
together with the inside
of her leatherette glove and
my jealousies together with
the innards of her leatherette
glut

they do this thing called
synchronized driving

i've come to the epiphany
that the country club makes
me wild

IV

and not at home exactly but
comfortable enough in my
surroundings:

a frog in a bathtub, say
hopping all the way to the
rim

all those bubbles, salts,
sponges

and people, two of them,

splashing about and
making my journey so
awkward and painful,

40

bashing my delicate
little legs, which i
kiss myself to make them
feel better

so maybe not so tough
as all that but chipper
and resilient and free

v

obviously
the brackish smell takes me back
to my childhood. which in itself is
part of the
enjoyment.

swallowing the urge to snap,
i spent hours and hours everyday
just watching people's ankles

both feet off the ground for the
serve, and then back in view,
balancing on a balletic toe,
before shunting off in the
other direction

the
better the player the bigger the
thrill. it's mesmerizing. and

all you can see is the shoes and
ankles.

you should try watching live tennis
your belly prodded with twigs

like, when i used to skulk around
the river bank, just next to the
courts

however much they convince
me that poplin check is the way to
go forward, i doubt they'll ever eradicate
my sock and trainer fascination

the rippling dimples of the grip

at one time i might have been a total
sucker for aertex. but i've been taught
since and have more sophisticated tastes

VI

measuring tape around
my neck, like a leash (which
i could chomp through
in 30 seconds flat but elect
not to)

him sitting there all smiles
on the dartboard shore,
his skin almost as crackled
as mine, from weeks and weeks
and weeks in biarritz, o-d-ing
on apricot kernel butter

sim in the corridor watching,
her bedroom timpanist
pulling faces to try and
get me to smoulder

the photographer saying yes
he thinks they probably do
have a replacement just in case

VII

not some trite antidote for brand
amnesia
this is essentially a love story

what i will say is this:
yes i have had an advance
for this book already
and the next

they're remaking 'hook'
you want to know if it's true

they've photoshopped
my midriff a touch

when the leftist runs snare
on the pastry sector

more grotesquely slick and
when i'm re-emerging even
when i'm going into rehab,
floating, in my own right...

who wears the cologne
in our relationship?

who has the rights to syndicate
the cartoons?

you want to know when the
resorts
whole luxury (or pretty much)
cars, parades, theme parks and
out into biscuit tins, soft toys,

you want to know if we'll end up
some sort of replacement
infantile monastery

scoops of baby and baby-sitter
crocs, to
identify with emotionally

somebody thought the public
needed a new figurehead, and
you think it's got something
to do with rené's death,
"giving me a voice, a personality"
to reinvigorate the brand

(serialization in
le canard enchaîné)
in book form
spilling my guts out

you want to know what marketing
genius came up with this plan

and you probably want to know
what i'm getting paid for it

peter saville redesigned me

redesigned me! me!
peter saville! me!

all he basically
came up with was a load
of tangled, squiggly lines

i took it as a compliment,
as you can imagine... after the
initial shock

and he says he
he knows so much
about those thoraxes

but more like what he'd look
like if i ever got hold of him
than what i look like

even on a bad scales day

in any case, i'm prepared to
let him have his day in the sun
basking in my reflected glamour

only problem would be if they
actually liked one of his designs
and wanted to adopt it
but that's unlikely

but i'll shuffle myself
undetectably under that bridge
when and if we come to it.

comes up to me in the snow –
I'm so cold and his arms are
stretched out wide as if he's about
to pop me like a crisp packet –
and I do feel I could burst –

I'm drawn to him like he's the
murderer in Stranger by the Lake.

– the inside of the foil's some kind
of complex deep diving bell in which the
pressure's been left running and suddenly
the port hole blows, flooding with air,
depressurising rapidly without the
necessary period of acclimatisation.

His hand smells like nail polish remover.
There's a tattoo of a sea gull right at the
top of his wrist. And there's a strange
moment when he first puts it into the bag.
The seagull stretches its wings full – span
and I go breathless, "caaaaaaaaaaaaaaaaw!!"

One or two of my vital organs shatter,
the beads of dried vinegar powder stinging
everything they touch.

I have no idea why I am still whispering.
I keep repeating to myself that it's
unlikely he's a murderer, just someone
who happens to know how to get what
he wants.

a whole quarter of an hour
in front of the mirror with
a faber no. 3 pencil and no
rubber. cool-doing-kitsch
satsuma with a hole in it
out of which you squeeze
or pour some other drink
like punches, pasteurized juices,
a watercress veloute, a mush-
room bisque or acquacotte.
the sparrows and the sparrows
raise hares like strays in horrible
conditions just for breeding so
that they can then be shot.
the hippos of the land are
greedy but only about one
thing which is the right to
be the first in the shower.
no early morning dental
appointment or viva will suffice
as reason to change the habit of a
hippo's life time which equals about
40–50 years. if you get a young one
try your best to act like its mate because
then you are in with your best opportunity
not to get your hopes up or anything.
extra curricular atrocities include
spelling program the american way,
building hot tubs in the manner of the
segal method, muddying boots and then
cleaning them off and sporranology.
this last a discipline that is much

mythologized because wearing sporrans
is especially difficult if you are a sparrow
or a sparrow.

in oversized Gaultier shorts:
will you ask them to come over?

It feels dangerous; yes, because
you want it. It feels fraudulent;
that's funny, I was thinking along
those lines too.

The sound of boxing shoes,
the sound of tapping a mic,
really uncertain and magical and
grownup, like you're suddenly
here and happy to say to the
whole arena that you're ready
to get the shit kicked out of you
but you're going to give as good
as you damn well get, while you
lost half your body weight for
the weigh in, the day before.

And anyway, they're models
not boxers though the distinction's
blurred. So will you ask them over?

They left already.

It depends on mood,
on occupation, on time of day.

Sometimes it's no good sitting
on chairs.

You sit in them, especially if
they're way too heavy
to move by yourself, so that
you have to accept how and
where they are and pile
things up around them.

The ideal?

Isamu Kenmochi's Kashiwado
chair, named after a sumo wrestler,
and almost as comfortable to sit in.

BUTTERMILK

Fill a heavy jar with double cream
shake and shake some more

or you can take whole milk,
add vinegar and leave a while

it's a choice between telling someone
you need them or setting the scene for
them to tell you

Let f and g be two functions
defined on some subset of real numbers.

Katherine Bernhardt's Nutella Waffle painting is on
the wall behind reception. It looks so unbelievably yummy.
The criss-cross of it is a reminder we're caught in a
T-Square. On the cafeteria cocktail menu coconut
came out as cocount.

Cumulant instead of semi-invariant,
the Naïve Kenysian subset
sets a Phillips curve beyond the clinic.

The floor is cork-effect and
packed with classy algorithms as far
as the nose can smell.
Hundredaire by Hey Willpower.

The ghost of [insert your first pet name]
touches its smooth magnetic strip scalding pink
against the machine beside the [something your pet was scared of]
and there's a strange show nobody'll ever get to see.

The rain punctures the ghost of [pet name again's]
hair. Blink. Quoting Milton Friedman said it was natural.

YOUR OVERSIZED RED CARHARTT SWEATER

Really elfish with those ultra tight black jeans

you walk into the gallery and are instantly
the most interesting and provocative thing

a dazzling ship in drydock, all tethered and
sleepy

which is of course including me, at the desk,
though I'm trying my best

typing without looking down
at my hands, all Nina Simone at Montreux,
glaring up and out and sometimes talking
all the while continuing with
the tune and song. A mix of 'Stars' and 'Feelings'.

She says all sorts if you watch the whole concert. It's
the one where if she was an ordinary person she'd embarrass
herself by shouting out to "her friend David", i.e. David Bowie,
who isn't there having said he would be. I've always hated him
a little for that,

but of course, there's little danger of embarrassing Nina Simone.

So at one point someone must get up from their
chair and make to leave and she just says "don't leave me"
really straight and flat.

trace the shape of the drop
and go over it

in a transparent object the
light behaves in a particular
way

let's say that the beams of light
come from the top left

then the darkest part will be
the left side as the light will

go through the drop and
illuminate the bottom right

on the left just under the
beam there will be a little
reflection if anything

down on the right will
be the most light part so

start shading the darkest
part using an "h" lead

it will cast a shadow on the
right side but in the middle
of it will be a light

then with a brush, smudge the
pencil for a more even finish

reinforce the shadow in the
vicinity of the drop

then smudge again

with a kneaded eraser pull some
reflection

then with a white pencil reinforce
the lines

it is dry like a sort of chalk

darken a little further

if you get black spots, try smudging
with a brush and if that doesn't
work then sharpen your eraser

sharpen it like an ant eater and
pull them off

then, if you have left any white spots
fill them in carefully with the lead

Salt all over
the path in
clumps. A clipped
helicopter bleat
hushes mourners
carrying the coffin,
suspended from it
as if by their
shoulder pads
all the arms
just beetling
eyelashes
with remarkable
steadfast pluck
as they plod out
a quarter pace
riverdance
of cherry tomatoes
on a shrink-wrapped
vine.

Place your left fingers on the keys S 5 G V
and your right fingers on the keys N 0 - =
Your thumbs should be on the space bar
Hold for 10 seconds

Place your left fingers on the keys § 1 C B
and your right fingers on the keys / J O 7
Your thumbs should be on the space bar
Take 8 deep breaths

Place your left fingers on the keys Z 3 X 5
and your right fingers on the keys M I U L
Your thumbs should be on the space bar
Hold for 30 seconds

Place your left fingers on the keys P O I U
and your right fingers on the keys 7 8 9 0
Your thumbs should be on the space bar
And relax

I am being held by a fire safety engineer;
the sort of fabric we are using is a kind of
boiled wool. We are wrapping the wool
around pieces of raw pork to simulate
human flesh in a tunic-type garb.

The light given off by this machine, not
to mention the heat, is powerful enough
to blind so we are putting on safety glasses,
standing well back, wearing lead vests and
sealing the area off from members of the
public. We are now going to heat the
package for 115 seconds.

The cloth is charred around the edges
from the tin foil but is very much intact. The
meat is cooked around the edges in a uniform
manner and though not terribly deep it's deep
enough to kill.

We've proven through this experiment that
your clothes can remain intact, even if you
actually die from heat exposure.

All day in the algae
dapple of the lamp.

We don't have a net.
Rubber gloves are so slippery
The only avenue is our hands.

My brother got all mean.

I'm stumped, afraid to touch them,
scared I will drop them.

What should I do?

Thanks for suggestions.
Please, no dumb answers.

Update: Fish seem fine.

When people say I'm a wallflower,
and it has been known, I take it as
a compliment, thinking of William
Morris's swirling golden lilies with
flecks of green and red or some kind
of new wallpaper that I just hope
someone licenses for someone else
to produce, which features Pierre-Joseph
Redouté's outrageously blue illustration of
Canterbury Bells, a blue so blue it's
pink around the edges, and if it was
on any old wall, it'd be so flower-like you
wouldn't hardly know the wall was there.

And now I'm thinking of another example,
some mosque tiles I saw once in Istanbul,
which were floral and geometric, but which
were so alive and fish-like they were unreal
and leaping gregariously out of whatever
pond or bowl they were kept in, an unfortunate
image in a way because they'd be leaping out to
their doom but whatever, let's say they were
swooshing about erratically like watercolour
when you dip your brush to clean it.

.

Crunchy wholegrain coated
in a delicious chocolate wrap
100% pleasure in snack breaks

A rolling eyeball keyring

A tray of finest plum tomatoes left
out in the sun

Crunchy wholegrain coated
in a delicious chocolate wrap
100% pleasure in snack breaks

A tray of Spanish blueberries

A bottle of Highland Spring plus
an Active Family Holiday to be won
certified by the Soil Association

A bag of baby spinach

Fairy Liquid

Diet Coke with Cherry

A tray of finest plum tomatoes cold
and clammy from the fridge

A tray of Spanish blueberries

Diet Coke

A bag of baby kale

Crunchy wholegrain coated
in a delicious chocolate wrap
100% pleasure in snack breaks

A tray of finest plum tomatoes
left in the bagging area

A bag of baby spinach

A bottle of Perrier water
with four hot air balloons on its label

A bag of dried beetroot

Two small tubs of cashews

A bag of chopped apple

Fairy Liquid Platinum

Diet Coke with Cherry

Crunchy wholegrain coated
in a delicious chocolate wrap
100% pleasure in snack breaks

A bag of baby spinach half frozen
in the fridge

THE NOVEL CAFÉ

So chilly in Beverly Hills! Much hushed!

Seen from above, there's just a floppy haircut
swooping (hither and thither) across the jungle path -
a serious contender for world's cutest rodent.

The air gets under your skin.
You know like how they make Peking Duck crispy,
blowing a thin atmosphere between your flesh and
the suddenly rubbery wetsuit that used to be
part of you?

The air's not just conditioned but shampooed,
expelled in millions of miniscule bubbles,

all whispering and simmering,
an open can of sparkling lychee
placed way too near your pillow.

        +++

A mega star's at home on a rare
night off, writing
stories, about possibly the greatest
living poets in the english language.

The plots are complex
and extensively borrow from
When Harry Met Sally and The Jungle Book
(but they boil down to this):

can a happy go lucky pop star
who has been getting a bit bored and restless of late
win the friend- and mentorship

of an internationally revered poet
and transform his life forever?

   +++

The path (which leads across the courtyard
from living room a to studio b)
is an enormous amorphous tongue
he walks across (tasting delicious).

It helps to come up with adverbs,
with plot triggers, with character names.

He's persistent but easily distracted.

In the courtyard itself, there's a pouf,
(some books,) two and a half cups of tea
& in the covered part there are rugs
on the wall.

A technical issue is how do they meet
but more important are the initial conversations
(the number swapping part) –

he wants to bypass his agents
(be taken seriously)

make some sort of claim –
distance himself from his neighbours.

It's this (and the lychee) that keeps
him awake (and the path, which is getting to be habitual)

to be honest sleep's out of the frame anyway because
the moon tonight's such a creep, so insistent
(such a whine), always papping away
(such an ass)

+++

He figures they have to have some reason
to get to know one another
(though he doesn't know why)
and makes it almost as clumsy and trite
as possible.

They are both going to be smelling the lilies
in the centre table of a gallery
somewhere hip, like Budapest, or Cagliari.

Their faces meet just like that
(both more interested in the flowers) than
the spaceman stuff on the walls.

Is Cagliari that hip? (Has he even been there?)
He knows enough
to know that it is now.

+++

It's coming very quickly
(the middle portion)
he's writing in email format
and throwing some texts in:

are you going to be at the 'not vital'
lecture at the Hammer Museum?

Dinner afterwards at the Novel Café?
I want to run some ideas past you

for my novel.

– Yeah we should do that. That'd be fun.
Did you try their tiger chai?

Pablo. Pablo please.
We're trying to talk
calmly to one another,
afraid of seeming alarmed,
and thereby sticking out,
like limpets on skerries,
hump-backed and paralysed,
letting it wash over us

abiding, and abiding.

To say we're stuck in a rut
would disservice
the rut.

I'm outgoing.
One day my friends and
I were at a shopping centre.

We developed an inside joke.

About unicorns.

It's been a secret
until now.

We doodle unicorns
on cards for each other
to mark special occasions.

And sometimes ask other
people whether they have
ever seen a unicorn in the wild
for dares.

Someone in our group,
their stepdad, who was
really good at making
rockets out of kitchen roll
tubes, he said:

This whole question
of The Unicorn Club,
I would stop that.

14 orange umbrellas, seen from above.
Tremble in the wind.
Eyes skid from one umbrella top to another,
like a giddy frog on a pond of lily pads.

The idea must be to avoid all the brolly
spikes, to tiptoe from one to the next
without being seen to linger. Trainers
soaked through, jean bottoms frayed.

Coin in pocket either a twenty pence
or a pound coin, thawing right forefinger
struggling to ascertain which. Individuals
crouch under all these lily pads still alive,

heads lift skyward, mouths open,
allow a few drops of rainwater to wet
lips and tongue. Gaze back to the lily pads,
prepare to re-inhabit the frog, and
continue saying what there is to say.

ACKNOWLEDGEMENTS

PRESS, BACK UP, HELP was first published as part of an artist-book *Open Wound in My Living Room* by printmaker Cat Outram, shown at the Royal Scottish Academy in 2015. 'Cool the Jets' and 'Mooc' were first published in the journal PARATEXT in 2015. '*Keats and Embarrassment* and Embarrassment' makes use of adaptation from Christopher Ricks' study *Keats and Embarrassment*. 'Crocodile' was first published in the journal *gorse* in 2014. 'Abuse Empowered Survive Thrive' was written before Craig David's recent resurgence.

Thanks Reuben. All the poets who come and have done to PiP, including: Nicky Melville, Iain Morrison, Ed Smith, Sam Riviere, Sophie Collins, Jennifer Williams, Samantha Walton, Graeme Smith, Jow Walton, Lila Matsumoto, Emilia Weber, Mike Saunders, Johnny Gallagher, Anne Laure Coxam, Jane Goldman, Greg Thomas, Daisy Lafarge, Thomas McColl etc.

Click and Collect
By Colin Herd

First published in this edition by Boiler House Press 2017
Part of UEA Publishing Project
All rights reserved
© Colin Herd 2017

The right of Colin Herd to be identified as the author of this work
has been asserted in accordance with the with the Copyright,
Design & Patents Act, 1988.

Design and typesetting by Emily Benton
emilybentonbookdesigner.co.uk
Typeset in Arnhem
Printed by Imprint Digital, UK
Distributed by NBN International

This book is sold subject to the condition that it shall not, by way of trade
or otherwise, be lent, resold, hired out, stored in a retrieval system, or
otherwise circulated without the publisher's prior consent in any form
of binding or cover other than that in which it is published and without
a similar condition including this condition being imposed on the
subsequent purchaser.

ISBN 978-1-911343-19-6